KT-165-643

Artists
Bob Bampton
Alan Male
Colin Newman
John Rignall

Cover
Steve Kaye

Acknowledgements

ARDEA, London: 12U (I Beames); 13U (V Taylor); 19U (F Gohier); 22U (H & J Beste); 22B (P Morris); 22UL (P Steyn); 22UR (A Weaving); 28BR (A Lindau); 30BL (F Gohier); 35B (F Gohier). **FRANK LANE**: 27B (A J Roberts). **NHPA**: 15B (A Bannister); 23BL (S Dalton). **NATURAL SCIENCE PHOTOS**: 25C (C F E Smedley). **OXFORD SCIENTIFIC FILMS**: 20U (G Merlen); 24U (R H Kuiter); 28UL (Z Leszczynski); 28BL (G A Maclean); 31B (D Thompson). **SURVIVAL ANGLIA**: title page (D Plage); 20B (M Linley); 23BR (J Foott); 28UR (M Linley); 30U (A Root); 31U (J & D Bartlett).

ISBN 0 86112 435 9

Published by Brimax Books, Newmarket, England 1987
Printed in Belgium
Third printing 1987.

ANIMAL LIFE

Staying Alive

Written by
Karen O'Callaghan &
Kate Londesborough

BRIMAX BOOKS · NEWMARKET · ENGLAND

Gentle giants

These giants of the animal world are not the deadly killers we might think. Some eat plants and others eat very tiny sea creatures.

Gorillas are gentle vegetarians. They do not harm any other animals to get their food. They feed on leaves, ferns, roots and shoots. Their food is so juicy that they never need to drink.

Elephants are plant eaters. They feed on leaves and grass. They can tear up whole trees and eat the leaves, branches and thorns. Their huge teeth are worn down by this rough food. In its lifetime an elephant will use up six sets of teeth.

This gigantic **blue whale** feeds on small sea creatures called krill. Instead of teeth, it has baleen plates that are like a giant comb. The whale swims along with its mouth open, trapping millions of krill between the plates. Then the whale moves its tongue to push out the water and swallows the krill.

krill

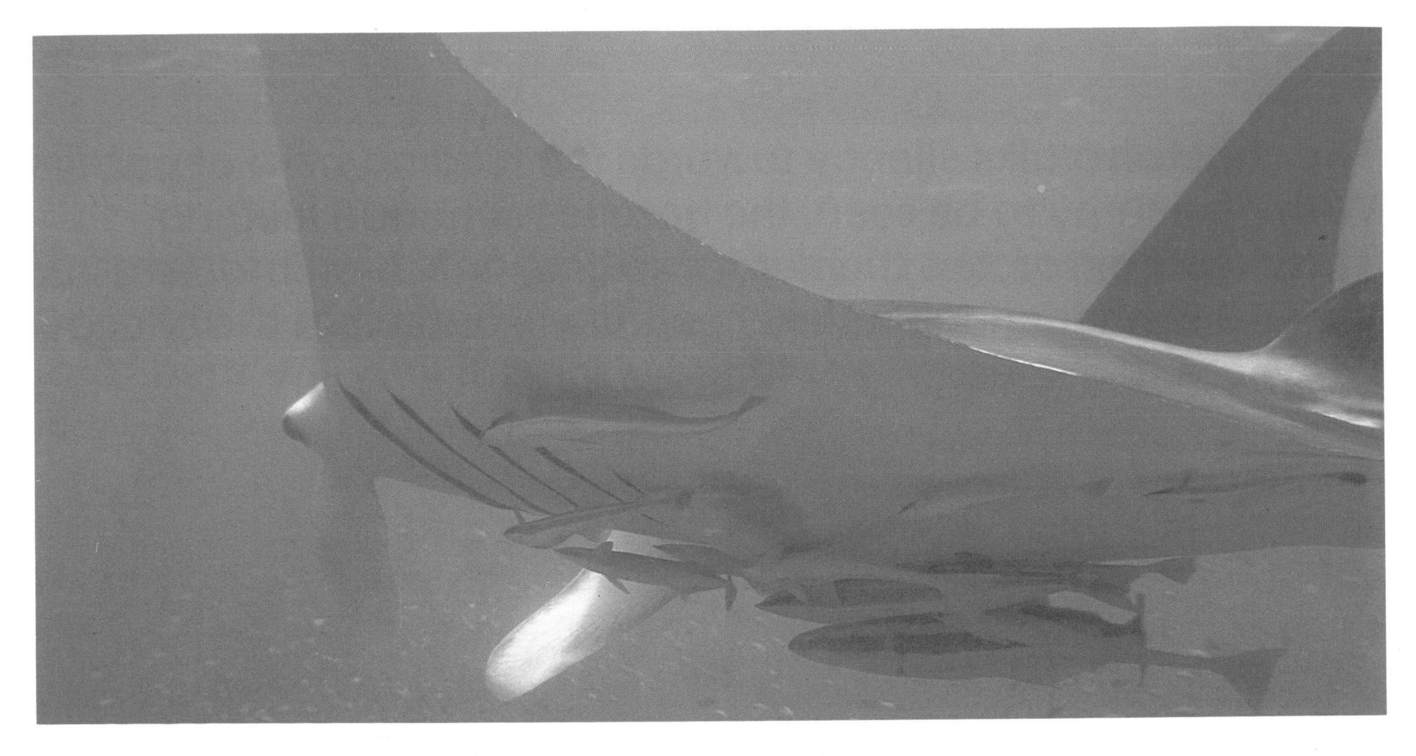

Most sea creatures are also safe from the **giant manta ray.** Although it looks fierce, it hardly ever attacks anything larger than a small fish. It feeds mainly on krill which it scoops up from the sea using horns at the side of its mouth.

Unusual feeders

These animals all have strange ways of getting their food. Some grow their own food. Some help one another in finding food.

Leaf cutting ants grow their own food. With scissor-like jaws they cut pieces of leaf and carry them back to the nest. The pieces are chewed up into a mushy pulp which is spread out to make a garden. A special fungus grows on this. The ants eat the fungus.

Marine iguanas are pestered by little insects called ticks. As the iguanas lie in the sun, **red rock crabs** crawl all over them eating the ticks. This is an easy way for the crabs to find food.

Whales are pestered by whale lice that dig into their skin and lay eggs. They swim to warmer seas where **phalarope birds** live. As the whales surface, the birds land on their backs to feed on the lice.

When the **great honey guide bird** finds a wild bees' nest, it calls to a **honey badger**. The bird leads the way. Using its sharp claws, the honey badger opens the nest and both feed on the honey.

Avoiding enemies

Hiding

Nature has given some animals special protection. The colour of their bodies helps them to hide from enemies. This is called camouflage.

The **gecko** is camouflaged against the bark of a tree. Because it is so difficult to see, the gecko can rest or sleep, safe from its enemies.

Lying very still this **viper** is nearly invisible on a bed of fallen leaves. Animals looking for food will not notice it.

Some animals can change their body colour to match their surroundings.

The **chameleon** can change colour. On a leaf it will be green. Against the bark of a tree it can change to red or brown. Not only is it hidden from enemies, the chameleon can also wait to attack its own prey without being seen.

plaice

squid

These sea creatures can also change colour to suit their backgrounds. When it lies on gravel, the smooth skin of the **plaice** becomes speckled to match the stones. The **squid** flashes coloured light patterns which confuse predators.

Other animals have special tricks to hide. They look like something else.

This **leafy sea dragon** could be mistaken for a piece of seaweed. All over its body, flaps of green skin dangle and wave as it floats through the water.

When a **leaf fish** is in danger, it stops swimming, turns on its side and floats. It looks like a dead leaf. It even has a short stump, just like a leaf stalk, on the end of its nose.

Hiding upside down among the spines of a sea urchin, the **shrimp fish** can avoid its enemies. The black lines along its body look like the sea urchin's spines, making it difficult to see.

The **giant peacock moth** has a pattern on its wings. The pattern looks like two large eyes. When the moth lands on a leaf, its wings carry on moving and the false eyes seem to blink. Because they look like the eyes of a large animal, enemies keep away.

On the end of this **puss moth caterpillar**'s body are special markings that look like a fierce face. If in danger, the caterpillar raises its tail to show the face. This frightens enemies away.

This **hairstreak butterfly**'s markings protect its soft body from enemies. On the back wings it has dots that look like eyes, and false feelers at the bottom of its wings. This looks like a false head. Attacking birds will peck at the false head and the butterfly will escape.

Warning colours

These animals do not need to hide. Their bright colours and markings warn other animals that they are dangerous to eat, and may have a poisonous bite or sting.

ladybird (ladybug)

arrow poison frog

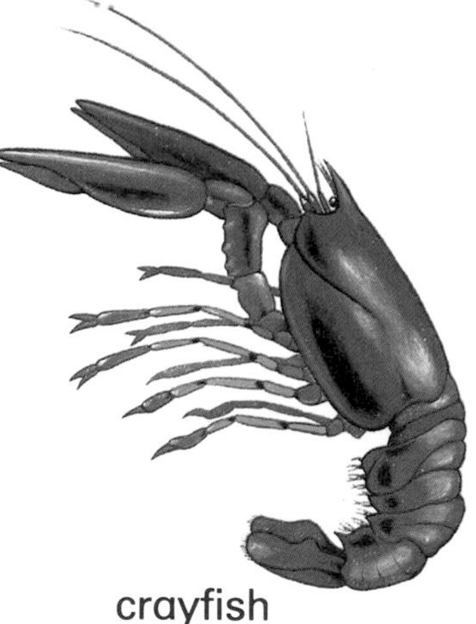

crayfish

ring necked snake

bee

sedge frog

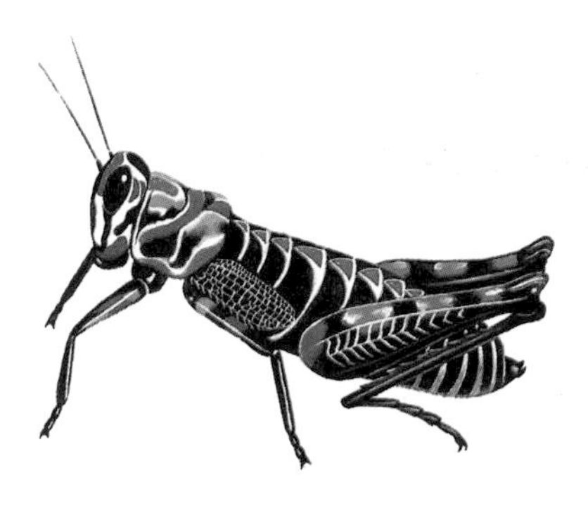

sunset grasshopper

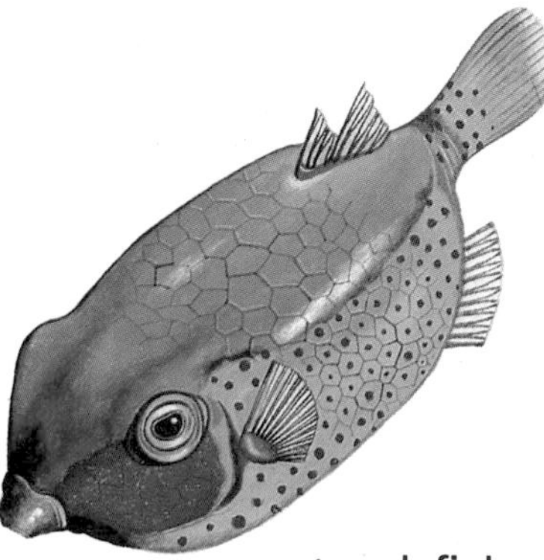

trunk fish

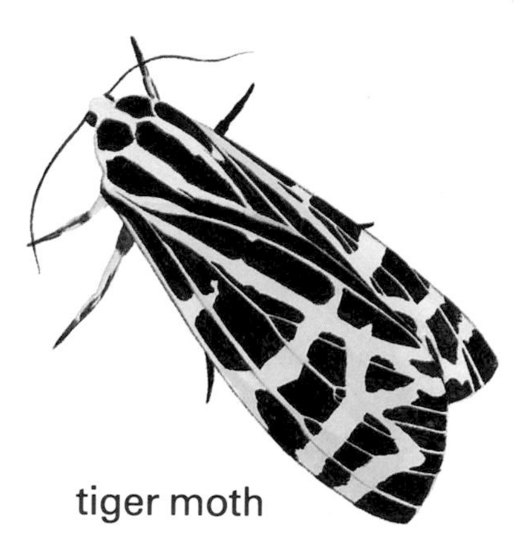

tiger moth

When the **shingle-backed lizard** is attacked, it cannot run away because it is so fat. Instead the lizard opens its mouth wide to show a bright blue tongue. Its enemies know that any bright colour means danger.

Burnet moths have a poison called cyanide inside their bodies. The moth's bright colours warn birds that it is unpleasant to eat.

Copying a warning

These animals are protected by their colouring in a different way. They copy nature's warning colours so that enemies will leave them alone. They are really harmless.

milk snake　　coral snake

The **milk snake** is protected from predators because it looks just like a poisonous **coral snake**. The milk snake is not poisonous at all but its enemies cannot tell the difference.

hoverfly　　wasp

The dangerous looking **hoverfly** is really quite harmless. It is safe from attack because it looks almost like a **wasp.** Predators think they will be stung if they eat it.

Copying a shape

Other insects are protected by their shape. They each look like part of a plant.

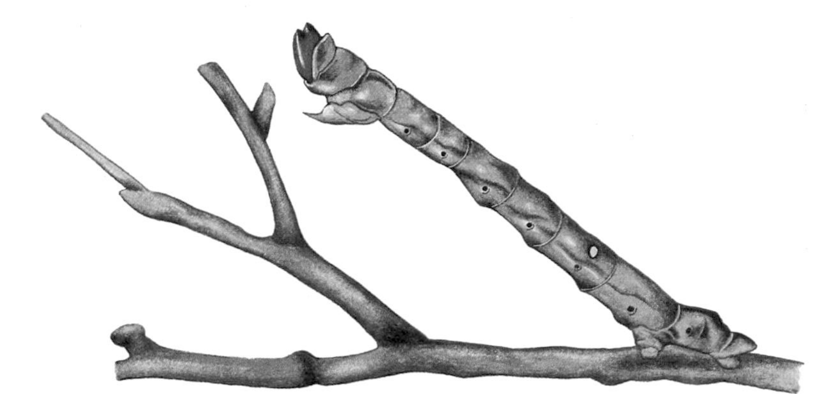

Animals are tricked by the **inchworm.** Standing completely still on a branch, the insect looks like a twig.

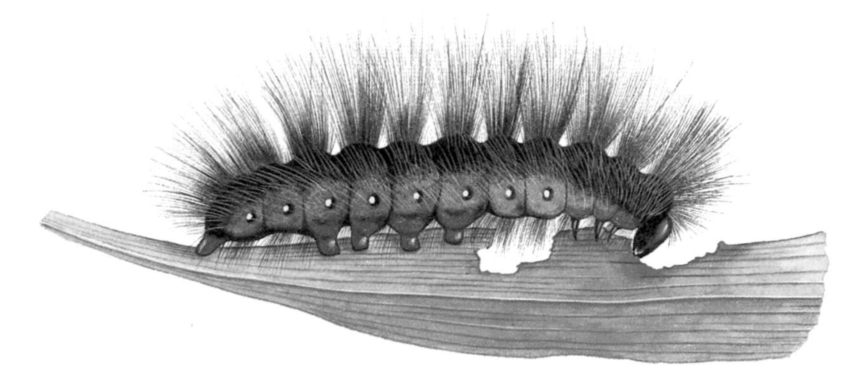

This **cryptic caterpillar** is covered in fine hairs. It could be mistaken for a fluffy seed blowing in the wind.

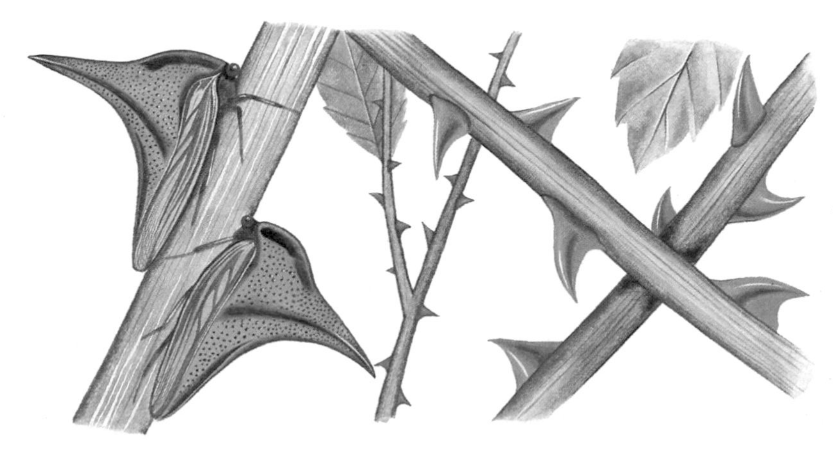

Living together in large groups, **thorn bugs** look just like the other thorns growing on this bush. They will not be noticed until they move.

Warning of danger

Animals are always on the look-out for danger. They have different ways of warning each other.

The **piapiac** (*pie-a-pie-ack*) and the **rhinoceros** have a special partnership. The bird clings on to the rhino's back, feeding on ticks. From this position it can see a long way. This helps the rhino who has very poor eyesight. If the bird sees an enemy it will call out loudly. It will even peck at the rhino's head to warn it of danger.

Prairie dogs have guards outside their burrows. They bark if an enemy appears.

As a warning, **rabbits** stamp on the ground with their back foot.

Elephants have a special way of keeping in touch with each other. They make soft rumbling noises in their throats all the time they are feeding. This noise stops immediately if an enemy is near. Silence means danger.

Bees use smell as a warning. Outside the nest, guard bees keep a look-out for any danger. If an animal comes to the nest, the guards give out a special scent (smell), whirring their wings to spread the smell. Other bees from inside will quickly come to help the guards protect the nest.

Defensive weapons

Many animals cannot escape quickly or hide away from their enemies. They need to defend themselves. Some animals have a weapon.

This **millipede** uses poisonous gas as a weapon. It has a line of little holes along either side of its body. The millipede will fire the gas at an attacker. When it is very scared the millipede shoots from all holes at once leaving behind a cloud of poison.

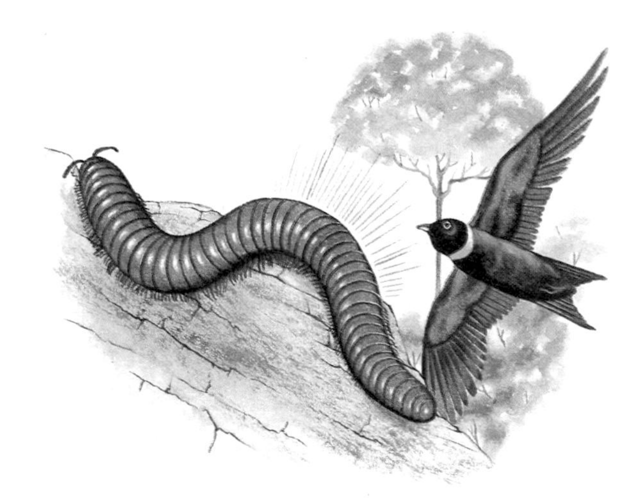

When it is attacked, the **skunk** squirts out two jets of liquid. This smells so disgusting that most animals run away. The liquid can also blind the skunk's enemies for a short time, giving it a chance of escape.

The **wood ant** squirts dangerous acid at any attacker.

The **black wasp** has a nasty sting which it uses if attacked.

When a **porcupine** is attacked it uses its quills as a weapon. First it shakes its body, rattling the quills as a warning. If the enemy does not run off, the porcupine turns round and charges backwards. It stabs the sharp quills into the animal's face. The quills break off easily leaving the predator full of painful spines.

Escape

Some animals escape from their predators.

If an **octopus** is attacked it squirts a jet of black ink out of a special tube called a siphon. Hidden by clouds of ink the octopus escapes. If it needs to move quickly the octopus can pump water through its siphon. This pushes it quickly along and out of danger.

Pronghorns are excellent runners. They live in the open grassland with nowhere to hide from predators. If they could not escape from enemies, pronghorns would all be killed off. When the herd is attacked by wolves, they run so fast that most of them escape. Only young, weak or sick animals are caught.

If a bird grabs this **lizard** by the tail, the tail breaks off but carries on wriggling. The bird is surprised and the lizard has a chance to escape.

When animals attack the **basilisk lizard** it escapes across the water. It can run so fast across the surface that it does not sink.

Other animals cannot escape by running away from danger. The **manatee** is a huge sea cow. It moves very slowly and cannot defend itself against enemies. It is safe because it lives in places that its enemies cannot reach. The muddy water is too salty for alligators and not deep enough for sharks.

Staying alive

All animals need the food that is in plants. If there were no plants, there would be no life. Some animals eat plants, other animals eat plant eaters. Each has its place in a food chain.

Staying alive is difficult for the plant eaters. These **dikdiks** live in fear of the hunters and must always keep watch.

Hunters do not attack animals just to harm them. This **fox** must kill to provide food for itself and its family.

Life is not always easy for the hunters. The **cheetah** must eat quickly or move its kill to a safer place. It may be stolen by a pack of **hyenas**. In large numbers the hyenas can overcome even the fiercest cheetah.

The **jaguar** has a better chance of catching a weak animal. The hunter is not always successful. Many animals escape!

Index